Mass Confusion

Why I Rejected The Church For So Long And What Changed

Susan R. Dolan

✽Berry Tree Press

Glenview, Illinois

Berry Tree Press
1509 Waukegan Road #1020
Glenview, Illinois 60025
www.BerryTreePress.com

Excerpts from Matthew Kelley's books are used with permission from Blue Sparrow/Wellspring/Beacon publishers.

ISBN 978-1-7376830-4-9 (soft cover)
ISBN 978-1-7376830-1-8 (eBook)
ISBN 978-1-7376830-3-2 (audio)

Special Editions
ISBN 978-1-7376830-2-5 (hard cover)
ISBN 978-1-7376830-5-6 (soft cover)

Publisher's Cataloging-In-Publication Data
(Prepared by The Donohue Group, Inc.)

Names: Dolan, Susan R., author.
Title: Mass confusion : why I rejected the Church for so long and
    what changed / Susan R. Dolan.
Description: Glenview, Illinois : Berry Tree Press, [2021] |
    Includes bibliographical references.
Identifiers: ISBN 9781737683049 (print) |
    ISBN 9781737683018 (ebook)
Subjects: LCSH: Dolan, Susan R.--Religion. |
    Catholics--Biography. | Spirituality. | Life change events--
    Religious aspects--Catholic Church. | LCGFT: Autobiographies.
Classification: LCC BX4651.3 .D65 2021 (print) | LCC BX4651.3
    (ebook) | DDC 282.092--dc23

Printed in the United States of America

For Evelyn and Joe

TABLE OF CONTENTS

PREFACE

I wish someone had given me this book when I was wandering in the spiritual desert . . . especially when I decided to return to the Catholic Church after 40 years—intimidated, self-conscious, full of doubts and questions, and overwhelmed by all that I didn't know about my faith. How I could have used a little guidance and empathy from a fellow traveler who understood my plight. Thankfully, I found helpful resources to guide my way. It is with a deep desire to "pay it forward" that I wrote this book.

Somehow, you've ended up with it in your hands. Maybe a friend gave it to you. Perhaps a loved one bought it as a gift for you to read. No matter how it came into your possession, I don't believe it's an accident. So, if you find yourself plagued by "mass confusion," may it forever be replaced by wisdom and peace as you explore the pages ahead.

Chapter 1

A Bad Catholic

If anyone should not be a Catholic, it's me. Despite being raised Catholic, I tried to stay as far away as possible from the Catholic Church. From a very early age, my parents somehow managed to instill in me a belief in God and a deep love for Jesus. In spite of their efforts, there were a lot of *good* reasons to call me a *bad* Catholic:

My first husband and I divorced. Check.

I mocked the Catholic Church. Check.

I joined another religion. Check.

I floated in and out of the Church over the course of 40 years, at my convenience, for all of the wrong reasons. Check.

Yet, as you'll read in the pages ahead, today I am a grateful Catholic. I wasn't actively searching for Jesus, but He never stopped pursuing me. Thank God.

Throughout my childhood, Sunday morning after Sunday morning, my father nagged me to get up and get ready for church. Between wake-up calls, I remember fantasizing that our family had gone to church and a helicopter had whisked me home, where I crawled back under the warm covers. Then my dad's final warning would blast me back into reality, "Snoozan! Last call—let's go!"

Starting around kindergarten, I vividly remember my father teaching me to pray. That stuck. And, at key moments growing up, I reached out to God for help and I received it. Even so, my parents had their hands full. A peek into my father's journal shortly after I turned 14 revealed what they were up against. My father described me as: "Sloppy with books and papers, arrogant and untamed, irresponsible, violating rules, insolent to mother, rude, selfish, and indifferent." (All true.) The entry ends with: *"YOU ARE GROUNDED! UNTIL FURTHER NOTICE!"*

I attended church with my parents throughout high school, but the drudgery and my complacency snowballed over time, even though I enjoyed Mass immensely when the cute boy from another parish visited our congregation. As soon as I enrolled in my hometown university and moved into a freshman dormitory, I stopped going. Only a few special occasions like weddings, funerals, holiday services, or to please my parents, led me to darken the doors of a church. Even then it felt like a ritual with no meaning. I rarely connected what happened at church with anything in my daily life; instead, I typically zoned out during Mass.

---

*Even then it felt like a ritual with no meaning.
I rarely connected what happened at church
with anything in my daily life;
instead, I typically zoned out during Mass.*

Despite my resistance to Catholicism in those years, two experiences—impossible to explain, yet undeniable—left an impression. The first was a powerful sensation I felt during nearly every Mass. Oftentimes, after Communion, a warmth and emotion would well up in me. I frequently fought back tears. When it happened, I would recall my father's words during my rebellious teenage years every time we walked out of church: "You feel better, don't you?" he'd ask.

"No," I'd say sullenly, refusing him the satisfaction of my real yes.

The second was two people: a parish priest, and a female professor at the university, a parishioner who rode her bike through campus and to church. They glowed with the brightest smiles I'd ever seen, no matter when or where I spotted them—as if they had an inner light source with no off switch. Their presence said more to me about spirituality than a thousand words from the altar. I'd wonder, "How can a person radiate such joy?"

Their presence said more to me about spirituality than a thousand words from the altar.

After graduation, my life took off. I landed my first full-time job as a nurse, attended law school at night, got married, gave birth to my daughter, then got a divorce.

When my daughter was a preschooler, I worked hard in a corporate law office and felt very sorry for myself. Late one night, thumbing through a magazine, I read an article about hospice and a review of Dannion Brinkley's book, *Saved by the Light*[1], detailing two of his near-death experiences. He said he had entered heaven and was sent back to earth to help the dying.

Now, I had no idea what a near-death experience was or what hospice workers did. Until then, the only dead body

I'd been near was my grandmother's. The idea of dealing regularly with death was unappealing in every way. Feeling a divine nudge, however, I called the local hospice care provider and offered to volunteer.

Throughout my two-decades-long career as a hospice professional, I was sure I would never return to the Catholic Church. Working first as a volunteer and then as an employee, I helped care for patients from many different backgrounds including Methodists, Lutherans, Presbyterians, Jews, Catholics, Buddhists, Baptists, Muslims, agnostics, and atheists. Witnessing countless patients draw their last breaths, I often wondered indignantly, "How could anybody put God in a box?"

I'm not proud of the fact that I referred to Catholics as "Mackerel Smackers," and mocked the exclusive "Catholic Club" during my tenure as a hospice professional. Or that I joked that going to Mass was like playing a game of Twister— kneel, stand, sit, repeat. Or that I took pleasure in telling how Saint Peter whispered to a Protestant man upon greeting him at the gates of Heaven, "Keep it quiet because we're walking by the Catholic section soon. They think they're the only ones here!" It felt good to push against what I viewed as a rigid, out-of-touch hierarchy.

Have you ever considered how the front and back of a beautiful tapestry differ? The front is exquisite, artfully displaying the unmistakable skill of the creator. At the same time, the back looks chaotic. Far from art, the muddled knots and threads reveal no discernible pattern.

Looking back, I now see how, for a far greater purpose, God was continually weaving together the people, events, and experiences in my life, even though, for decades, I was oblivious to His subtle handiwork. Mired in self-pity, I stared woefully at a jumble of knots and loose threads—events and circumstances that appeared disjointed and unrelated— unaware that throughout this spiritually frayed period in my life, the Master Weaver was at work. For much too long, I was fixated on my own important agendas, focusing intently on the back of the tapestry.

Looking back, I now see how,
for a far greater purpose, God was continually
weaving together the people, events,
and experiences in my life, even though, for decades,
I was oblivious to His subtle handiwork.

Chapter 2
A Good Start

My mother describes my father as "the best Catholic I've ever known." She credits him with nurturing my faith and assuming much of my everyday spiritual training with one-sentence lessons.

"You know not the day nor the hour."

"If you don't care who gets the credit, you can get a lot done."

"Don't hit a child; it's not a fair fight."

"Teasing is a disguised insult."

My parents met in 1949 at a summer camp just north of New York City. Mom was the camp nurse on hiatus from nursing school; Dad was the social director. He had just graduated from Manhattan College, a private Roman Catholic liberal arts school in the Bronx that he attended after WWII. He served in the war as a Navy pilot on the USS Essex aircraft carrier.

Mom says she was drawn to my father because he was older and mature, accustomed to sacrifice, and intent on making a positive difference in the world. "His faith in God drew me in the most—his deep commitment to follow the Gospel and serve the poor," she told me. "He was different from any man I'd ever known." She said she'd never met anyone who tried as hard to be Christ-like, which inspired her to convert to Catholicism. In fact, she was so taken by what she learned about the Catholic faith before her marriage that she considered becoming a nun.

Despite being as poor as church mice before they married, Mom says my father talked about starting a foundation for "the poorest of the poor." Long after his death, his dream came to fruition.

When my mother's father learned that my dad had proposed to my mom, my grandfather said, "We have nothing against him, but we don't want you to marry him." Pop-Pop refused to go to the wedding because my father was a Catholic and my mother was raised as a Protestant. My grandmother, "the fixer," told her husband, "Audrey can get along without us, but can we get along without Audrey?" One of my favorite family photographs shows my handsome grandfather, smiling in a tuxedo, at my parents' wedding.

In addition to his devotion to God,
my father was a good and humble man
with a deep love of his family and the underdog.

In addition to his devotion to God, my father was a good and humble man with a deep love of his family and the underdog. Dad tried to see the best in everyone. I remember feeling uncomfortable and yet mesmerized when he'd offer rides to strangers standing in the rain. He called checkout clerks by their names and always found something nice to say. I marveled at their reactions of surprise and delight.

My father's reputation as a university professor, therapist, and skilled facilitator resulted in numerous awards, publications, and national recognition. As his reputation grew, religious communities in turmoil increasingly sought his aid. He traveled extensively to counsel priests and nuns who found in his demeanor the freedom and acceptance to express their true feelings, rethink their vocations, and reshape their futures, enabled by Dad's spirit of acceptance, safety, and reconciliation. During this time, he stepped onto the national stage as host of the NBC television show *Guideline*, which focused on contemporary topics involving the Catholic Church.

My mom describes my dad as a rebel because when he witnessed what he believed was an injustice, unfairness, or cruelty, he would speak up. For example, when the university administration pressured him to change the failing grades of students on the football team so they could play, he refused. As a result, he was unpopular with many people. My mother once confided that one of my dad's coworkers told her, "Your husband can be a real asshole." Candidly, I would be surprised if that was the only epithet used to describe him.

Like even the most saintly,
Dad was a complex and often conflicted man.

Like even the most saintly, Dad was a complex and often conflicted man. He had a dark side that sometimes surfaced when bouts of depression would drive him to disappear into the basement or otherwise withdraw for days. During those periods, his devastating criticism loomed large. We dreaded the moments when he would pull forth a list of our shortcomings. He'd accurately enumerate our latest misdeeds and tell us how disappointed he was, ending with a lecture about what he expected in the future. I gave him a lot of good material.

One of my dad's favorite sayings was borrowed from Calvin Coolidge: "Nothing in the world can take the place of persistence. Talent will not; nothing is more common than unsuccessful men with talent. Genius will not; unrewarded genius is almost a proverb. Education alone will not; the world is full of educated derelicts. Persistence and determination are omnipotent."[2] Throughout my life, I saw my father's diligent efforts to follow Jesus and strive to do the right thing, no matter the cost.

Another favorite maxim we often heard Dad say was, "We shall *under* come." The statement reflected his persistent and determined effort to take the road less traveled, love his neighbor, and turn the other cheek—things he was honest about struggling with his whole life.

. . . my father orchestrated a number of events like this in an effort to fuel our budding faith.

One of my earliest, most vivid memories was when my father took us to a convent. The nuns gave us unconsecrated hosts used for Communion. The flat sheets, made from flour and water, fascinated me. I poked out each circular host, leaving a large, Swiss-cheese-like edible wafer. We took the hosts to our neighbor's house, where we were excited to reenact Mass. In retrospect, I see that my father orchestrated a number of events like this in an effort to fuel our budding faith.

Our long oval dinner table welcomed many guests. Often, it looked like a meeting of the United Nations, encircled by foreign students and lonely souls my parents had invited to our home. Small talk bored my dad, so he sought ways to avoid it. He would introduce unusual and exciting topics, gently guiding a conversation from gossip and politics, football scores, or new restaurants to questions of faith and morality.

Once, he invited guests to name the event in Jesus's life they would have most liked to have witnessed. One guest answered, "At Gethsemane, when Peter cut off the servant's ear and Jesus healed him instantly."

Another guest chose the wedding feast at Cana. "All that wine!" she laughed.

"Any miracle to reassure my imperfect faith," sighed another.

Answers inevitably prompted another round of stimulating questions. "What would the ideal church be like? What does Jesus ask of us when we are in great conflict? What is the ideal church community? How do we achieve it all?"

"What is the best and worst part of religious life?" Dad once asked a Benedictine monk during dinner.

"The best is the rigorous training of the mind," he replied. "I received a superb education in Europe and at Catholic University." Then he paused, sighed, and said, "The worst part is celibacy."

No one fell asleep at our dinner table.

My mother's influence in my life was no less profound than my father's. Her quiet strength and faithful presence undergirded us all. Mom started her professional life as a registered nurse and teacher, and later became a clinical

11

psychologist. She practiced for more than 30 years or, as she says, "Until I got it right."

My mother's influence in my life was no less profound than my father's. Her quiet strength and faithful presence undergirded us all.

Believing that people have tremendous capacity for growth and change, she devoted her life to being part of the process. When my mom and dad graduated on the same day from Columbia University's Teacher's College with doctoral degrees, the *New York Daily News* grabbed the story. Dad created a miniature graduation gown for my five-year-old brother (as an 18-month-old, I was too tiny for academic attire), my parents donned their caps and gowns, and the photographer snapped away. "You'll be on the front page tomorrow," he promised. But the first monkey launched into space took off the next day and our family was bumped to the paper's midsection. Though temporarily upstaged by a furry primate, my parents went on to become extremely accomplished in their respective fields, authoring numerous books together on child development and family life.

When I consider how my mother and father influenced me, I think of the following quote, often attributed to Saint Francis of Assisi: "Preach the Gospel at all times. When necessary use words."

A Good Start

Long before forgiveness became a common topic in everyday life, my father was writing a book on the subject. Before its completion, he died of a massive heart attack at the age of 61. Only now am I fully appreciating who he was, how much he meant to me, and what a profound effect he has had on my life.

After I graduated from college, I visited my parents every weekend. On the Sunday before Dad died, he was resting in bed, fatigued after shoveling snow off our long driveway. We were celebrating because I had just received a letter of acceptance to law school. As I sat on the bed, he took my hand and said, "If I never see you again, I want you to know how proud I am of you." I remember feeling confused and uncomfortable. Of course he'd see me; I visited every weekend. I was not to see him alive again. At that time, I had no inkling that the dying often sense the time of their death.

"*Preach the Gospel at all times.*
When necessary use words."

CHAPTER 3
THE REAL WOO-WOO

My hospice career gave my life purpose and taught me profound lessons. Death is the great equalizer. When someone faces the end of life, everything changes. The trivial falls away. What seemed significant becomes insignificant: titles, awards, degrees, skin color, looks, the car you drive, the size of the house you live in. A sort of triage occurs; you don't want to waste precious time. The focus is on what is most important: your loved ones, life review, your relationship with God, and what the afterlife may hold.

During this time, I studied New Age healing techniques; visited psychics and mediums; attended self-help classes, seminars, and conferences; read countless books; and joined another religion, all in search of something elusive. I was excited to explore new ideas, beliefs, and spiritual practices, but they were unsustainable. When I'd tell my mom about my "woo-woo" experiences, she would politely respond, "Oh sweetie, I just go straight to the Source."

No matter what I did, I couldn't shake an undercurrent of restlessness.

I remember thinking, "I have a job I love . . . I'm helping patients and families . . . my daughter is happy and healthy. So why do I feel so unsettled?" No matter what I did, I couldn't shake an undercurrent of restlessness.

Shortly after I joined hospice, I reunited with a long-lost flame. The chemistry had been there during college, but geography and circumstances intervened. Though each of us had married someone else, I never forgot him. His name was Steve. Seventeen years later, when he and I were both single parents, mutual friends reconnected us. We locked eyes and I had the same overwhelming feeling I did when we first met. Two years later, my daughter and I moved from Wisconsin to Chicago, where Steve and I married and blended our families.

Our new life together started off smoothly enough, but troubled waters lay ahead. We were naïve to think our love for each other was enough to carry us through the challenges of blending a family. The struggles were much harder than we could have imagined.

I continued to take on more responsibility with hospice, adding to the stress in our home. I remember crawling into bed one morning after an on-call visit. I kissed Steve hello at 2 a.m. and at 4 a.m. I kissed him goodbye as I rolled back out of bed to make another visit.

Desperately seeking significance,
I doubled down on my need to work
harder and better, hoping increased achievements
would lead to peace and satisfaction.

Steve supported my career and was proud of me, but inevitably the demands of my work became unmanageable. When family members raised concerns about my unrealistic schedule, I'd explain, "I have important work to do!" In retrospect, I was saying, "Don't you know how important I am?!" Desperately seeking significance, I doubled down on my need to work harder and better, hoping increased achievements would lead to peace and satisfaction.

One of my fellow workaholic friends dubbed Sunday evening "the new Monday morning," and that's how I rationalized working every Sunday. I told myself that as soon as I "caught up" at work, I'd honor the Sabbath, but that never happened. If I'd been honest, I would have acknowledged that burying myself in work was a way to avoid the uncomfortable feelings and issues surrounding my personal life and constantly pushing beyond my limits was harmful, not heroic.

Eventually, Steve and I talked things through and I resigned my position. It was a big decision to step away from a job I'd had for so long and worked on so hard, but I couldn't deny I was a workaholic and that I was burned out.

"Is this all there is?" I'd continue to wonder. I was searching for something I couldn't see or put into words. Little did I appreciate at the time that the Catholic faith is full of mystery and supernatural happenings—miracles, the Holy Spirit, answered prayers, angels, incorruptible saints, earthly visitations by the Virgin Mary, grace, peace, love, Jesus, and death and resurrection—the real *woo-woo*.

Little did I appreciate at the time that the Catholic faith is full of mystery and supernatural happenings.

Though I longed to connect to something greater, no matter how hard I tried, I could not sit in church with so many questions and resentments. I was restless, bored, in a fog, and impatient to escape.

CHAPTER 4
CRASH AND BURN

It's said that God moves in mysterious ways. For years I thought that was a nice cliché, but looking back on my life, I know that it's true. If you'd told me after a divorce from my first husband, a bumpy second marriage, turning my back on the Catholic Church, and joining another religion, I would return to the Church after 40 years, I would *never* have believed you.

I'd always believed in God, loved Jesus, and tried to be a good person. I just couldn't make sense of Catholic dogma and the Mass. Though I longed to connect to something greater, no matter how hard I tried, I could not sit in church with so many questions and resentments. I was restless, bored, in a fog, and impatient to escape. For a brief period I went to church to appease Steve because he felt so strongly about our attending Mass as a family. And I continued to pop in and out of church over the years, with varying degrees of commitment.

Shortly after a family blowup, a friend of Steve's gave him a copy of the book *Rediscover Jesus* by Matthew Kelly. Then, as my husband read the book not once, but over and over—more than 17 times as of this writing—I began to see him transform. He started getting up at four o'clock every morning to spend an hour praying, reading and meditating. Matthew Kelly refers to this time as "the classroom of silence,"[3] an indispensable ingredient of the spiritual life because "clarity emerges from silence."[4] He explains, "The world is noisy and distracting. It is in the silence that we find God and our true self."[5]

Steve softened. He was kinder. As his behavior continued to change, I grew more interested in what he was doing, reading, thinking, and feeling—and curious about Matthew Kelly and the organization he created, Dynamic Catholic.

Around the same time, I accepted another job in the healthcare field, which I enjoyed, especially for the opportunity to regularly sleep through the night. Soon after that, my mother moved from California to Illinois. Then, shortly after settling in a retirement community close to our home, she fell and broke her hip and I began visiting her in the rehab center every day after work.

A problem that began as a hairline crack had somehow widened into a canyon. But I was tired, and this time I gave up.

And then it happened. On the Saturday before Easter old trouble resurfaced between Steve and me. A problem that began as a hairline crack had somehow widened into a canyon. But I was tired, and this time I gave up. I said to myself, "I'm leaving." My mom was my first priority, I reasoned, work was second, and finding another place to live and leaving Steve was third. Even as I set my list, I had no energy to get to number three because all my resources went to helping care for my mom and to keeping up with my work.

Certain that our marriage had reached the point of no return, I let Steve know I intended to move out and that I had an appointment to look at an apartment. The news hit him hard. With great difficulty, he began to talk, and then he broke down and cried. For the first time, I saw the problem through his eyes, too. Our relationship was only one battleground. We both also battled within ourselves and had our own scars . . . but I was worn down and worn out.

Around this time, a classmate from years before, a beautiful and faith-filled single mom, came to mind. I'd remembered her because of a story she once shared with me. After her young husband died unexpectedly, she met a good and kind man who loved her, but she did not love him. Overwhelmed with raising her daughter alone, and with work and school, she told me she prayed constantly for God to turn her heart around for this stable suitor. Although hesitant, she felt that if she did accept his proposal, God would answer her prayer. I remember the day, after we both graduated, that she and I reconnected. Greeting me with a huge smile, she described answering her door one day to look into the eyes of the patient man she had fallen deeply in love with. She accepted his proposal and told me, "God turned my heart around!"

Although I was often guilty of being a Convenient Christian—mindful of Jesus when life became challenging or when I had time to work Him into my agenda—I decided to try again. So, I prayed every day for God to turn my heart around for my husband.

I decided to try again. So, I prayed every day for God to turn my heart around for my husband.

21

Steve and I agreed to visit a marriage therapist who helped us frame our struggles with compassion for both sides, and she convinced us that resolution—healing, even—was possible. After covering a lot of ground in months of therapy, we found ourselves beginning to hope. "If I had to predict, I would say that you two will stay married," our therapist told us. And I continued to pray every day, "God, please restore my love for my husband because I can't do it by myself."

Steve started sharing inspiring emails with me every morning from Father Richard Rohr, a Franciscan priest. One message read, "Transformation has little to do with intelligence, willpower, or perfection. It has everything to do with honest humility, willingness, and surrender."[6] I remember thinking we couldn't change the past, but we could move forward together with forgiveness and create a new future.

Not long afterward, during the period when we were still involved in weekly marriage therapy, Steve called me at work. He had just received an email inviting him to a Dynamic Catholic "Passion and Purpose" event with Matthew Kelly in Milwaukee and he asked if I'd like to attend. I was intrigued by Steve's excitement and interested in learning more about the man who was profoundly influencing my husband. To my astonishment, I also sensed God saying: "It's time for a change, Susan. You've been working too hard; you haven't made enough time for Me."

This event would change our lives.

CHAPTER 5
A DYNAMIC CATHOLIC

Following a productive marriage counseling session, we were walking out of the therapist's office and headed to the Matthew Kelly event when Steve exclaimed, "Look!" while pointing to a double rainbow. We took it as a positive sign. Guided by our skilled therapist, we were learning to open up to each other in a new way. Despite many painful moments, we could express how blessed we felt to go through this ordeal and still be together.

Looking back, I could not have been in a better place to receive Matthew's message. Between the therapist's wisdom, a beautiful evening, and the changes happening in our lives, I was primed to hear what Matthew had to say.

We pulled into the parking lot feeling as if we'd just entered the orbit of a major sporting event. Cars streamed in from as far as the eye could see. Policemen were directing traffic. Crowds of people were hurrying into the arena. An exciting buzz filled the air as smiling greeters welcomed us with genuine warmth.

When I saw people wearing "Be Bold. Be Catholic." T-shirts, I was flabbergasted. I'd never seen Catholics so outspoken in their faith. Walking inside, I was surprised to see the auditorium overflowing with thousands of people.

When I saw people wearing
"Be Bold. Be Catholic." T-shirts,
I was flabbergasted.

A gifted musician filled the venue with beautiful songs. Looking around, I noticed a man onstage, to the side, wearing jeans and boots. He sat in an armchair and seemed to enjoy the music as much as the crowd. Then he got up, moved to the center of the stage, and spoke with gravity and grace. The man was Matthew Kelly. As he spoke, we laughed, we cried, and we sat captivated for hours. At times, you could hear a pin drop.

"Get excited about your faith," he said. "If you're not, you don't understand it." I'd never been excited about Catholicism. To be honest, I knew little about my faith. Matthew invited us to discover the "genius of Catholicism" by summarizing many of the good things the Church has done over the centuries. He told us how the Catholic Church has fed, educated, housed, and cared for more sick people, and visited more prisoners, than any other institution in the history of humanity.

"Get excited about your faith," he said.
"If you're not, you don't understand it."

Amidst the crowd's positive response, Matthew demonstrated Dynamic Catholic's motto, *"Meeting people where they are . . . Leading them to where God calls them to be!"* Instead of preaching, Matthew educated us about the Catholic faith in a deeply touching way I could understand and relate to. It made me want to learn more. He seemed able to connect with people of strong faith like my husband, fallen-away Catholics like me, disengaged Catholics, reverts, converts, agnostics, atheists, and everyone in between.

When Matthew asked, "What will your life look like 10 years from now?" I recognized that constructing a response could be life-changing. Rather than continuing my hamster-wheel-style work habits, I was intent on discerning God's path for my future. Was I willing to surrender my plans and discover more about His? Despite my uncertainty, I knew one thing for certain: I didn't want another decade to mindlessly pass me by.

Matthew explained that many of us are afraid of silence and solitude. Even so, we need time to sit with God and figure things out so that we can make great decisions in our lives. He promised that, while initially it might be difficult to carve out this time each day, eventually we would guard it like a lion. Before you know it, he told us, you'll be in regular communication with God and relying on Him before acting. In other words, we'd develop a meaningful prayer life.

Prayer is going deep into the classroom of silence because that's where we hear the voice of God.

But what, exactly, is prayer? I wondered. *Is it more than asking God to supply what I want and need?* Prayer is going deep into the classroom of silence because that's where we hear the voice of God. If we don't start our day with prayer, chronic busyness in our lives will crowd God out. In *I Heard*

God Laugh, Matthew wrote, "Busy is not our friend. It makes us feel overwhelmed, tired, and inadequate. If busy were a person, would you spend all day with that person today, and then all day with that person again tomorrow?"[7] Matthew's antidote to the "poison of busyness" is prayer. "Prayer inspires us to live with great intention and avoid wasting our lives. Busy drags our lives out of focus. Prayer brings our lives into focus." He recommended my new favorite prayer: "God, what do you think I should do?"[8] Now, I pray for diligence and vigilance to reorient myself throughout the day to stay focused on asking God what He thinks I should do. Because my big fancy plans, with me in the starring role (instead of Jesus), hadn't worked out so well.

Matthew assured us that, sooner than later, this practice would become a habit and profoundly affect our level of peace and serenity throughout the day, and we would become the best versions of ourselves. What should we do when we find ourselves stuck and unsure of the path forward? Simply "Do the next right thing," he wisely advised. As you do, the next step will become clear. Put together enough small "right" steps and you'll be on a productive path.

He challenged us to read five pages of a great spiritual book every day to engage in lifelong learning. At that rate, we could read at least 10 books every year and potentially hundreds of inspirational books or more over the course of our lives. A book can change a life. Having seen how Matthew's book, *Rediscover Jesus*, changed my husband's life, I was motivated to follow his suggestion.

What if he's right? I wondered.
What if God really loves me?

Listening to Matthew, something within me profoundly shifted. I wanted what he had. I wanted to be part of the same faith that inspired his authentic spirituality. *What if he's right?* I wondered. *What if God really loves me? What if He has an amazing purpose and plan for my life? What if He is writing my story from His perspective? What if the front of the tapestry, the side God invites us to see, is the only one I should gaze upon, and with gratitude?*

When Matthew invited us to pray a prayer of transformation, I thought, *What have I got to lose?* Today, I consider this profound prayer to be a cornerstone of my spiritual journey:

> Loving Father,
> Here I am. I trust that You have an incredible plan for me. Transform me. Transform my life. Everything is on the table. Take what You want and give what You want to give. Transform me into the person You created me to be, so I can live the life You envision for me. I hold nothing back; I am 100 percent available. How can I help?
> Amen.

In *Rediscover Jesus*, Matthew wrote about this prayer of transformation: "If you want to see miracles, pray that prayer. If you want to see and experience miracles in your own life, pray a wholehearted prayer of transformation. That's a prayer God will answer. God always answers a prayer of transformation. Never once in the history of the world has God not answered a sincere prayer of transformation."[9]

My prayer was answered;
God turned my heart around!

As it turned out, I was no exception: One evening, shortly after the Passion & Purpose event, I looked at my husband with fresh eyes and remembered why I'd fallen deeply in love with him. My prayer was answered; God turned my heart around!

At the same time my spiritual transformation was in full swing—and while I began attending Mass with intention for the first time in my life—my mother was angry and heartbroken over the Catholic Church's sexual abuse crisis.

My father always seemed able to balance his awareness of the frailties, flaws, and foibles of those who comprise the Church with an equally profound awareness of its divine mission. Dad often said to "hang loose in the structure and beware of manmade laws." I reminded my mom of this and two of my father's favorite quotes. The first is from Frank Sheed: "We are not baptized into the hierarchy, do not receive the cardinals sacramentally, will not spend an eternity in the beatific vision of the pope. . . . Christ *is* the point. . . . Even if I sometimes find the Church, as I have to live in her, a pain in the neck, I should still say that nothing a pope, [bishop, priest, or cardinal] could do or say would make me wish to leave the Church, though I might well wish that [they] would leave."[10]

And my mom smiled knowingly when I read her the second quote, this one from the early twentieth-century Catholic writer, Hilaire Belloc, as cited in Bishop Robert Barron's book, *Letter to a Suffering Church*. "The Catholic Church is an institution I am bound to hold divine—but for unbelievers a proof of its divinity might be found in the fact that no merely human institution conducted with such knavish imbecility would have lasted a fortnight."[11]

As Mom and I continued our discussion, her spirits rose. Some of our best conversations continue to revolve around our ever-evolving faith.

While I'm the first to admit that I rejected the Church because of my misperceptions and misunderstandings, I see now that what I considered the problem was actually my only solution. I was quick to write off Catholicism when I didn't understand my faith. Today, by contrast, Catholicism has evolved from being a strange and stuffy word to a daily adventure.

I was a Swiss cheese Catholic: holey (not holy).

Sell your books at sellbackyourBook.com!

Go to sellbackyourBook.com and get an instant price quote. We even pay the shipping - see what your old books are worth today!

Inspected By:adela_sanchez

00039981371

0003998 1371

CHAPTER 6

A SWISS CHEESE CATHOLIC

Of the 1.7 million Catholics baptized each year, 22 years later, only an estimated 150,000 are still in the Church.[12] Eighty-two percent of Catholics in the pews are disengaged to some extent.[13] These statistics described me to a tee.

From outward appearances, many would have assumed I was an engaged Catholic as I attended church with my husband. They may have thought, "There's Susan Dolan. I saw her picture in the parish directory. Her husband is a pillar in our church. She's a hospice worker. Susan is a good Catholic." And they would have been wrong. I attended Mass not to worship God, but to support my husband and, at times, for professional reasons: to give hospice updates or follow up on a parishioner whose loved one had died.

I sat in the pew thinking about what to fix for dinner, and what I'd need for work the next day. My recurring thought was, "I cannot wait until this is over!" I loved Jesus and dreaded church. In short, when I did attend Mass, I was not all in. I was a Swiss cheese Catholic: holey (not holy). We appear so stoic in church. We stand, kneel, and sit at the same time, pray at the same time, and sing at the same time. It's sometimes impossible to tell whether Catholics are worshiping or checked out, as I was most of the time.

It's sometimes impossible to tell whether Catholics are worshiping or checked out, as I was most of the time.

For as long as I can remember, Mass confused me. Fearful of how others might judge me for asking questions, I maintained a "Don't ask, don't tell" policy. God tried to get my attention, but I was too stubborn and prideful to care. After my faith was renewed, the scales fell from my eyes. Finally, I could appreciate the beautiful Catholic church across the street from where I worked. I felt as if that church was calling to me. When I finally summoned the courage, after so many years, I attended Mass there. For the first time in my life, I entered a church in awe. I marveled at the beautiful artwork and stained glass. I inhaled the intoxicating smell of incense. I grew intensely curious about the lives of the saints throughout church history, recalling an Oscar Wilde quote: "The only difference between the saint and the sinner is that every saint has a past, and every sinner has a future."[14]

Today, as I grasp the beauty of the Mass from a historical perspective and delve into its mystery, things come alive for me, like extraordinary time travel. I attend the Last Supper with Jesus and hear His command, "Do *this* in memory of me." The Eucharist and the thought of connecting with the powerful Person who created the cosmos overwhelm me.

It's been said that "going to church doesn't make you any more a Christian than going to the garage makes you a car."[15] These days, I do more than show up and expect to be inspired. I've learned to prepare for Mass by studying related scripture verses, including the Old Testament readings, Psalms, and the Gospel.

Following Matthew Kelly's advice, I also started reading the Gospels each day. Matthew describes the Bible as "pure genius . . . the most complete spiritual manual, and the best way to live."[16] After reading a multitude of self-improvement books, I was ready for the real thing. Much to my surprise, I became keenly interested in learning more about how the Old and New Testaments fit into one big, exciting, overarching love story. I discovered that the Bible is not in chronological order; rather it's like a library containing multiple books written by many authors at different times in history for a variety of reasons. Yet, miraculously, all 73 books harmonize.

After reading a multitude of self-improvement books, I was ready for the real thing.

Reading and listening, I wondered, "How could I have ignored the greatest stories ever told?" Better than any Hollywood script, the Bible has something for everyone: love, hate, sex, power struggles, betrayal, battles, torture, forgiveness, grace, wisdom, sexual abuse, inspiration, mystery, miracles, healing, redemption, demons, death, and resurrection. In truth, I never took the Bible seriously because I was intimidated by it and assumed it was boring. It is not. In fact, it's filled with fallible people whose "hurts, hang-ups, and habits"[17] are just like yours and mine.

Ananias lied about his income. The Samaritan woman was married five times before living, unwed, with a sixth man. Peter denied Jesus three times. Rahab was a prostitute who ended up in Jesus' direct bloodline. Paul viciously persecuted Christians before encountering the risen Jesus and experiencing a dramatic conversion. King David committed adultery, arranged for the death of his lover's husband, and looked the other way when his son raped his daughter. Moses was a murderer. And that's just for starters.

The spiritual practices I learned through Dynamic Catholic have also made a difference in the time I spend alone with God each day. Growing up, when my mom would get antsy and crave a change of scenery, she called it Restless Butt Syndrome—RBS. Years ago, when I tried to pray or meditate, I'd get a bad case of RBS. Today, it can still take some time for me to settle down and enter into the "classroom of silence." However, as I incrementally built more time into my morning routine, what began after the Milwaukee event as five minutes a day has expanded into a transcendent, unhurried time. Matthew was right: I now guard this time ferociously.

One of my biggest regrets is the decades it took for me to understand and appreciate my faith. When I expressed this remorse to an older friend, she exclaimed, "You're lucky to have discovered the genius of Catholicism so young!" Her response is a powerful reminder that everything occurs in God's time—something I know, and forget more often than not.

It pains me to think how I deprived my daughter of the treasures of the Mass as she saw me resist Catholicism for years. I attended church as a mind-numbing, painful, and mechanical experience of my own making because I didn't understand it and had no desire to learn about it. Thankfully, I've been able to forgive myself for this unfortunate blunder and I trust that God has forgiven me too.

My faith and experience of the Mass today are completely different. These days, when I enter a church it feels like a cherished and sacred sanctuary. There are no outside distractions; it's peaceful and calms my heart, mind, and soul—like a spiritual retreat. Most importantly, I often hear the voice of God.

At Mass, I worship and pray to God, sing praise, give thanks, confess my sins, ask for forgiveness, grant forgiveness, celebrate my faith in community, and offer my gifts. I spend time in stillness and reflection. At the end of Mass, I'm challenged, as the original disciples were, to "go in peace to love and serve the Lord."

One of my favorite parts of the Mass experience is using my Mass journal. Matthew encourages taking a journal to Mass and, before church begins, praying, "God, please show me through this Mass one way I can become a better version of myself this week."[18] Then, I listen for the voice of God. ". . . Until people are listening to the voice of God in their lives, they are simply incapable of absorbing the Scriptures, the Sunday homily, CCD class, adult education courses, great Catholic books, and the phenomenal beauty of the sacraments," Matthew explains.[19] Long after I began work on this book, I reviewed entries in my Mass journals for a two-year period and discovered an entry I'd forgotten: "It's time to write my book. Come follow me."

After I returned to church, I was surprised to discover a multitude of people in my community who also were "fallen-away Catholics" and "reverts" like me. I learned about a pastor, deacon, and seminary student who all had returned to the Church after many years. A friend I'd known for a long time, a pillar in her church and community, returned after decades. Another woman, the director of a large Catholic education program, reappeared after a years-long absence. After hearing more and more of these stories, I remember thinking, "Wow, I'm not alone!"

My hope is that, as you read this book, you might consider attending Mass again with a docent (a fellow human being or the Holy Spirit) to rediscover why the Gospel is truly Good News. I recommend visiting a parish with a radical focus on hospitality to make you feel welcome.

I'm grateful to say I'm no longer a Swiss cheese Catholic. I know that a loving God never left me; I left Him.

After I returned to church, I was surprised to discover a multitude of people in my community who also were "fallen-away Catholics" and "reverts" like me.

CHAPTER 7
OLD WORDS . . . NEW MEANINGS

Many people live with a sense of restlessness. They're searching for something, but unsure what it is. They're not truly happy, grateful, or at peace. My mother, the psychologist, would ask clients, "How's that working for you? Would you consider trying another way?" Saint Augustine of Hippo wrote of God, "Our heart is restless until it rests in you." I can attest to that as one who lived with a restless heart for most of my life.

As a result, I was put off by many terms I heard in church: sin, repentance, and evangelize, to name a few. Looking back, I wonder, "Why were they so offensive to me?" These days, when I encounter something that I don't understand or that may be difficult to accept, I pray, read, ponder, and take time to research and learn. Sooner or later, I receive insight. In the past, I blamed God or "stuffy" religion for my lack of understanding. Now, I ask myself if I'm making a humble and honest effort to discern with an open heart and mind. And by the grace of God, I continue to see many things in a new light.

The word *sin* used to bother me, for example, but *sin* simply means "to miss the mark." When I'm unkind, impatient, judgmental, self-absorbed, or greedy, I'm not the best version of myself; I've missed the target. For a long time,

I was reluctant even to say, "I'm a sinner," because I wanted to be perfect. It was embarrassing to admit my countless faults. Now, I accept that I will never be perfect and that I am a sinner. All of this helps me grow in humility and continually ask God for help.

The word *repentance* bothered me, too. It felt overbearing and threatening, like a fire-and-brimstone sermon or a fiery street preacher holding up a condemning sign. In my arrogance and ignorance, I didn't know that *repent* means simply to try again. Repentance is a change of mind that leads to a change in actions. Instead of seeing this as an ultra-religious or "churchy" term, it's my opportunity for a do-over—to acknowledge how I messed up, ask God for help, and choose a different direction.

Asking for help took on new meaning when I read the story of Jim Woodford's near-death experience in his book, *Heaven, an Unexpected Journey.*[20] I've long been drawn to near-death stories, not only because they led me to work in hospice, but because they remind me that there is a God, there is life after death, and that what our culture values is quite different from what God values.

The chapter titled "An Exchange of Yokes" begins with a scripture passage from Matthew 11:28-30: "Come to Me, all who are weary and are heavy-laden, and I will give you rest. Take My yoke upon you and learn from Me, for I am gentle and humble in heart, and you will find rest for your souls. For My yoke is easy and My burden is light."[21]

Woodford was an accomplished career pilot with no time for God. After his near-death experience, he explained, ". . . there was an exchange of yokes in my life. Where I had the yoke, the control column of an aircraft in my grasp from an early age, now the yoke of Jesus came upon me. It meant that God was now leading me. . . . It is a yoke of walking together with Jesus under a yoke of love. It is not a yoke of more stuff or striving . . . it is a yoke of friendship, grace, compassion, hospitality, love, joy, and constant presence."[22]

In the past, hearing this scripture passage from Saint Matthew, I envisioned oxen, beasts of burden, weighed down by huge, restrictive, wooden yokes. When I read my husband this excerpt from Woodford's book, he said taking on God's yoke is like holding His hand—another ah-ha moment for me. I love the idea of being "yoked to God," holding His hand as He teaches, comforts, protects, and guides me.

It's like a starving person
discovering a limitless food source
and sharing the find with other starving people.

The word *evangelize* used to evoke images of someone pounding an angry fist on the Bible. Now I know it means to share the Good News about Jesus. It's like a starving person discovering a limitless food source and sharing the find with other starving people.

Talking about evangelization, Bishop Robert Barron, founder of Word on Fire media ministry, said, "We should think of others not as objects to be used, or annoying people in the way of realizing our projects, but rather those whom we are called to serve. Instead of saying, 'Why is this annoying person in my way?' we might ask, 'What opportunity for evangelization has presented itself?' Has God put this person in your life precisely for this purpose? Think of an annoying person in your life and reflect on what opportunity God might be putting in your way for evangelization, which begins with love."[23]

Bishop Barron introduced me to an electrifying concept of the Church as a dynamic living organism (not an organization) called the "Mystical Body of Christ"—a prolongation of Jesus' mission and presence across time and space. Jesus, the head of the Church, sent the Holy Spirit to continue and preserve His Church by unifying the apostles, disciples, and all who follow Him, to change the world. We are organisms—spiritual beings with souls—all connected and part of the Mystical Body of Christ commissioned at the end of every Mass to share the life-transforming good news of the Gospel. Wow![24]

Jesus welcomes everybody; He excludes no one.

The origin of the word *catholic* is from the Greek term *katholikos*, combining two Greek words: *kath* meaning "throughout," and *holos* meaning "whole." "Throughout the whole" includes *everyone*. Jesus welcomes *everybody*; He excludes no one. He especially reaches out to those on the margins: outcasts, thieves, strangers, tax collectors, prostitutes, the poor, the sick, adulterers, and criminals. I feel at home now in the Catholic Church remembering that we are all children of God.

Bishop Barron teaches that genuine contentment comes from doing what we were made to do: order our life to God because we are wired for God. When we match our God-given gifts, talents, and skills with the needs of our world, intending to make it a better place, we experience true happiness. In simple acts of love, we connect to the power that created the cosmos, because God is love. Making this connection is the secret of life!

*If you are skeptical or feel far from God,
my encouragement is to start with prayer,
the quickest portal to God.*

CHAPTER 8

PRAYER TIME CHANGES

Catholics say a lot of prayers. The Mass is full of prayers. People who report near-death experiences often describe prayer as tangible energy and recount seeing these requests for help arrive in Heaven immediately, like beams of light.

Throughout Scripture, we're told that help may not come when and how we want it, but it will come. That said, our chances of receiving help increase greatly if we ask for it through prayer. If you are skeptical or feel far from God, my encouragement is to start with prayer, the quickest portal to God.

When I need help—and fast—my go-to prayers include my mom's all-purpose "Lord show me the way and give me the strength." A favorite emergency prayer, borrowed from author Anne Lamott, is: "Help me help me help me. Thank you thank you thank you." Or, I may pray, "Come, Holy Spirit. Please give me Your wisdom, humility, compassion, patience, grace, and peace (whatever I need most in that moment)." My number-one prayer is, "God, what do you think I should do?" Every time that I remember to stop, take a deep breath, ask God what He thinks, and then listen, my shoulders relax, I slow down, and receive an answer.

Howard Storm leads people in prayer, but this was not always the case. Years ago, he was an atheist who had a near-

43

death experience. He cried out for Jesus to save him and was rescued by spiritual beings. While he was experiencing what's called a Panoramic Life Review (a time when you see your whole life's history in great detail, including every emotion and also the emotions of those with whom you interacted), Howard wanted God to notice all the awards he'd received while working as a professor. God told Howard He didn't care about the accolades. He wanted to know how Howard had treated his students. Howard had been mean, even cruel, to them. He changed his mind about the existence of God and who Jesus is. No longer an atheist, he has written books about his experience and, since, has served as a pastor for many years. These types of stories are not uncommon.[25]

At the "Passion and Purpose" program, Matthew Kelly challenged us to dedicate time to prayer every day because, "It changes your whole day—your whole life." When we put our phones away, turn off the news, and grow quiet and still, we make room to hear God's voice. Matthew compares prayer time to atomic energy. "[It's] a contraction that produces an expansion," he says. "We draw back from the world (contraction) so that we can live more fully in the world (expansion)."[26] Each morning when I pray, my day seems to expand, allowing time for everything I need to do.

Even as a girl, I knew something sacred was happening as I watched my father pray in church. I recall his deliberately making the sign of the cross as if in slow motion, whispering: "In the name of the Father, and of the Son, and of the Holy Spirit. Amen." He might also make the sign of the cross on my forehead as we talked at the dinner table, or when I walked by. The sign of the cross, itself, is an ancient and powerful prayer that feels like a dynamic, spiritual embrace.

The sign of the cross, itself,
is an ancient and powerful prayer
that feels like a dynamic, spiritual embrace.

My father loved The Lord's Prayer, which has been described as a summation of the whole Gospel:

> Our Father, who art in heaven, hallowed be thy name. Thy kingdom come, thy will be done, on earth, as it is in heaven.
> Give us this day our daily bread and forgive us our trespasses as we forgive those who trespass against us.
> And lead us not into temptation, but deliver us from evil.
> Amen

My dad wrote his own version of the Our Father, which hangs in our home today:

> Accepting Parent of all, who dwells here and apart, may all our thoughts and words affirm your holiness.
> May your desires for peace and harmony be fulfilled and may everyone live as morally in this world as they do in the next.
> Provide what we need and overlook our serious offenses but only to the extent that we do the same for others.
> Don't make our lives more difficult without purpose, but protect us from all harm.
> So be it.

In *Rediscover Jesus*, Matthew asks a life-changing question: "Prayer changes everything. It is impossible to get close to Jesus and stay close to Him without developing an intimate daily conversation with Him. The habit of daily prayer will transform you in unimaginable ways and you will wonder how you ever lived without it. We can survive without prayer, but we cannot thrive without it. Are you thriving or just surviving?"

Here's how Matthew describes the prayer process that I now follow every morning:

- Gratitude: Begin by thanking God in a personal dialogue for whatever you are most grateful for today.

- Awareness: Revisit the times in the last 24 hours when you were and were not the best version of yourself. Talk to God about these situations and what you learned from them.

- Significant Moments: Identify something you experienced in the last 24 hours. Explore what God might be trying to say to you through that event (or person).

- Peace: Ask God to forgive you for any wrong you have committed (against yourself, another person, or Him) and to fill you with a deep and abiding peace.

- Freedom: Speak with God about how He is inviting you to change your life, so that you can experience the freedom to be the best version of yourself.

❧ Others: Lift up to God anyone you feel called to pray for today, asking God to bless and guide them.

❧ Pray the Our Father.[27]

Early one morning during my quiet time, I read a quote from Father Richard Rohr: "A mature Christian sees Christ in everything and everyone else."[28] This reminded me that, just weeks before, I'd come across my daughter's response to a question from her catechism teacher. She was in grade school at the time. The teacher asked, "What does God look like?" and she answered, "He looks like nothing, and He looks like everything. He is in the eyes of a cat or a dog. He is in the wind and the trees."

These thoughts were fresh in my mind as my husband called me out to our driveway. He had jacked up his car and removed the front wheel on the driver's side. He pointed to a little furry head peeking out through an opening in the driver's-side wheel well. We locked eyes with a tiny, frightened, wailing kitten. The night before, Steve had returned home, tired after a long day. He was puzzled because he thought he'd heard a cat on the 15-mile drive home from work. However, he dismissed the sound and forgot about it altogether . . . until the next morning when he started his car and the meowing resumed.

Something rose up in me. "This is Christ kitty!" I whispered. My heart swelled as I prayed while trying to entice him out from underneath the car with tuna fish. Lying on the ground for hours, silent, still, and patient, I saw myself in that skittish little kitten. I thought of God waiting for me—coaxing, loving, encouraging, never giving up—finally leading me back home to Him.

Reflecting on Christian maturity, Fr. Rohr goes on to say, "A mature Christian sees Christ in everything and everyone else. That is a definition that will never fail you, always demand more of you, and give you no reasons to fight, exclude or reject anyone."[29]

When I make God my top priority through a robust prayer life, everything else falls into place.

Recently, I heard someone say, "Make an appointment with God every day and keep it as if you were meeting with the most important person in the world." Prayer is an instant means to re-center my sinful self when I become selfish, lazy, judgmental, prideful, and lose focus on what is most important. When I make God my top priority through a robust prayer life, everything else falls into place. Whereas, if I get busy with emails, phone calls, or errands and start my day off preoccupied with my to-do list, I feel as if I'm going through the day running on empty rather than relying on God.

"So I tell you, whatever you ask for in prayer, believe that you have received it, and it will be yours." (Mark 11:24, NRSV).

And what became of Christ kitty? He was adopted by my loved and admired neighbor, Mary, also known as "the Cat Lady."

CHAPTER 9

HANG LOOSE IN THE STRUCTURE

When I decided to return to the Catholic Church after 40 years, I felt like a salmon swimming upstream because I came back in the midst of some of the most serious allegations of the Church's sexual abuse crisis. Ironically, I found comfort in my father's words written over five decades ago.

> *If I want the Catholic Church to change*
> *and the people in it to change, I must change first.*
> *Personal change must come from within.*

While writing this book, I rediscovered an unpublished manuscript titled *Forty Years of Catholic Childhood* that my father completed in 1967. He wrote, "I was prepared to solve all the problems of the modern church. But the logistics of changing the behavior of all those foot-dragging bishops, priests, and laity was more formidable a task than even I was prepared to undertake. To save the trouble and expense of phone calls and chancery conferences and round trips to Rome, I decided to modify my own attitudes and behavior." He continued, "The practical implications of free choice for man and for me became disturbingly clear: If I want the

Catholic Church to change and the people in it to change, *I must change first*. Personal change must come from within. If I am in a church that I would like to see changed, the best place for me to start is with myself because I am the only member of the Church who is likely to change as a direct result of my own efforts."

As I try to keep my focus on Jesus, the failures of the Church come into perspective. I don't excuse or minimize them, but I remember that the Church is made up of imperfect people. It has gone through trials and tribulations for centuries and continues to exist because of Jesus. Like my father, I can say, "I love Jesus Christ. For that reason, I am committed to His Church while it limps toward eternity." So, I strive to hang loose in the structure when, despite horrific scandals and flawed human beings, I remember that I am a member of the Church founded by Jesus over 2,000 years ago.

To be sure, I certainly see the irony: here I am quoting my father about the Catholic Church when, previously, I would've disagreed with him and mocked the sentiment. Now, I find myself echoing my parents, and understanding that behind their love for me was God's love.

My parents used to read aloud to me my favorite childhood book, *Are You My Mother?* by P.D. Eastman. This keepsake reminds me of my search for God. The story begins when a little bird emerges from an egg and falls out of the nest while its mother is away searching for food. Walking along to find her, the baby bird encounters a kitten, hen, dog, cow, boat, plane, and large bulldozer (the "Snort"), each time asking, "Are you my mother?" And every reply is "No." At the end of the book, the Snort lifts the terrified baby bird high into the sky and gently deposits it into its nest.

Ending where he began, the little bird sees its mother and exclaims, "You are a bird, and you are my mother!"[30] In a similar journey, I grew up in the Catholic Church, left the Catholic Church, rejected the Catholic Church, and thought I'd never return to the Catholic Church. But here I am, thanks to the grace of God.

*I grew up in the Catholic Church,
left the Catholic Church, rejected the Catholic Church,
and thought I'd never return to the Catholic Church.
But here I am, thanks to the grace of God.*

CHAPTER 10
ENDING THE CONFUSION

As I reflect on my journey, I believe God is graciously allowing me to glimpse parts of the pattern He's been weaving throughout the tapestry of my life. Stitch by stitch, I'm starting to see how He has taken each bad decision and wrong turn and—instead of giving up on me—has given me "joy and gladness instead of grief" (Isaiah 61:3, GNT).

If you're someone who likes to read the end of a book first, here's a CliffsNotes version of why I rejected the Church for so long and what changed. For as far back as I can remember, the Mass made no sense to me, and for longer than I care to admit, I did nothing about it. I'd close my mind, never considering what Sunday mornings might mean to the rest of my life, leaving me in an endless loop of seemingly senseless Sunday rituals. Week after week, year after year, I sat at a feast and went home hungry. In my ignorance and pride, and for too many years, I left it at that.

And though I loved my family and my work, put on a happy face, and occasionally sensed a Divine connection through prayer, I felt unsettled and restless. My "pressing" to-do list was my priority. Often sliding into self-pity, I saw my life as a swath of uneven fabric, all knots and broken threads, never guessing that the other side comprised a beautiful tapestry woven by God, start to finish.

And all the while, God never left me; the Master Weaver was at work.

Then, in the throes of an uncertain marriage, my husband and I sat, enthralled, at a Dynamic Catholic event led by Matthew Kelly, and the random threads of my life began to form a pattern. *What if Matthew is right?* I let myself wonder. *What if God loves me? What if He sees all that I can't, and by gazing at Him, I can better see what He sees?*

Steve and I have both discovered that when we live a God- and prayer-centered life, our marriage thrives.

What came next began with my husband, as he practiced what he read in a book by Matthew. Every day, my husband got up earlier and earlier to study, meditate, and pray, in what Matthew calls the "classroom of silence," set apart from the noise to hear God and make sense of the world. In Steve's life, a day at a time, I saw a radical change. As an unexpected gift, Steve and I have both discovered that when we live a God- and prayer-centered life, our marriage thrives.

What God, through Matthew, did for my husband and me is what I pray this book now does for you. God pulled back the curtain on His divine feast, whetting my appetite to embark on an exciting journey of spiritual growth, starting with a lesson on silence.

Until we have enough quiet to hear our Creator, and ourselves, how can we know who we are? Or why we're here, and what matters? Silence and prayer, the opposite of busy, are life's great reset. In them lie the answers to "God, what do you think I should do?" Pursued long enough, in silence and prayer, we find the best of ourselves. As a result, we soon come to jealously guard this special time.

To see and experience miracles in your own life, pray a wholehearted prayer of transformation. As Matthew Kelly says: "That's a prayer God will answer."

As my faith came to life, I grew aware of the tapestry. I came to the feast with new hunger. The physical church, for example, the building, began to call to me. Increasingly, the traditions to which I'd been exposed since childhood were infused with new meaning.

I began to see that the power that created the cosmos and became an infant could also come to me in the Eucharist. And something else: instead of going to church to be inspired, I began to prepare for church, to be a steward of all it could teach me.

---

*"How could I have ignored
the greatest stories ever told?"*

"How could I have ignored the greatest stories ever told?" I'd wonder. The Bible cuts no corners on human nature or on God's love. On Matthew's advice, I began to read the Gospels, piquing my interest to know how the Old and New Testaments interplay—and do they ever, which explains why "The New Testament lies hidden in the Old and the Old Testament is unveiled in the New."[31] I began a Mass journal to hold what comes to me during Mass. After only a few pages, the things I write down talk back to me.

I'm part of God's agenda now, no longer the star of my own. Whether my days are good, or good and challenging, they belong to a plan far superior to anything I could devise. I trust them to God, relieving myself of a great burden!

Once I recoiled from the Mass; now I cherish it. Once I saw church as an endurance test; now I know it as sacred time, a holy mystery. Once I used the time in church to plan my week. Now, I listen for the voice of God.

Writing this book has brought the contrasts in my life back into sharp relief. Years ago, if you'd told me that I would return to the Church and love being Catholic, I would have shaken my head and rolled my eyes. But the tapestry God weaves looks messy only from the underside, and I no longer believe in accidents.

If you're holding this book,
you have an invitation to come home.

If you're holding this book, you have an invitation to come home. God is not condemning you; He only wants to save us from ourselves. His gentle invitation bears repeating: "Come to me, all you that are weary and are carrying heavy burdens, and I will give you rest. Take my yoke upon you, and learn from Me; for I am gentle and humble in heart, and you will find rest for your souls" (Matthew 11:28-29, NRSV).

Could you use that rest? Pray and ask for help. From any of many sources, or at a local parish, discover a docent in the faith, someone to guide you into discovery, and come to the feast.

Your tapestry has another side.

Epilogue
Calm in the Storm

In the midst of completing this book, the COVID-19 global pandemic turned the world upside down. The new coronavirus infiltrated the Chicagoland area as my mother was hospitalized shortly before her ninety-second birthday.

I remember where I was and what I was doing when the space shuttle Challenger exploded and when the Twin Towers collapsed on September 11, 2001. Likewise, I remember exactly where I was when the nurse at my mother's retirement community called me at work to say, "Your mother is in an ambulance on the way to the COVID-19 hospital."

Tears streamed down my face as I stood up from my desk. The room swirled in slow motion. "How could my frail mom possibly survive this vicious disease after her recent stroke, fall, and concussion?" I wondered, anguished. Walking out of my office, I couldn't anticipate how much my faith would deepen in the coming months.

By God's grace, despite a long list of symptoms, my mother wasn't placed on a ventilator, the hallmark of the worst cases. Because the hospital allowed no visitors, I could only talk with her by phone. When I did, a distant, faint voice begged me, "Get me out of here, Susan, please . . . " She didn't really understand what was happening, and it broke my heart.

Hospital protocol required "fever-free" status for at least three days before discharging a COVID-19 patient. Just when I thought she was recovering, evening would come, and like clockwork, her temperature would spike, restarting the 72-hour clock all over again. I felt helpless.

Mom's primary care physician, although an employee of a large secular healthcare system, assured me with the comforting words, "I believe in God, and I believe God will take care of your mom." These words became my mantra, reminding me that God has a plan and has everything covered. My one job is to trust Him, so I continued to pray for my mom. Trust God, pray, repeat.

Days of coughing, pain, fever, confusion, and no appetite left my mom depleted. In her years as a clinical psychologist, she would ask her patients, "How is your spirit?" When I asked her this question, she replied, "Diminished—but I still have my faith."

I felt an increasing urgency to get Mom home. From my years as a hospice worker, I could not bear the thought of her dying in the hospital, separated from family. Though her fever still spiked, thanks to the efforts of a seasoned hospice nurse, hospital administrators discharged my mother early. Because of my nursing background, they accepted my promise to give her full in-home care with the help of a local hospice. Eight days after going into the hospital, my mom came home.

Early in my hospice career I learned, with humility, not to predict when a patient would die.

Early in my hospice career I learned, with humility, not to predict when a patient would die. God has His timing. As the body weakens, I believe the spirit grows stronger. People who appear as though they might die soon often defy predictions. They are on their own timetable, perhaps attending to unfinished business in this world.

I repeatedly predicted my mother's death, witnessing what I considered obvious end-of-life symptoms. She slept most of the time. Her appetite for food or fluids disappeared. Her breathing was labored. She was restless, agitated, reviewed her life's major milestones, and apparently had what hospice professionals refer to as a "last hurrah"—a final burst of energy.

After many days of near-constant sleep, nibbles of food and sips of water, Mom sat up in bed on Holy Saturday and exclaimed, "I want sausage!" So on Easter morning, alert and happy, she walked to the kitchen table and ate everything on her plate: two eggs, four links of sausage, toast, fruit, orange juice, and tea. Then, she had fun on the telephone wishing her family a happy Easter.

Hospice workers believe that the last hurrah is a brief respite, like a long-distance runner who somehow summons the power to push across the finish line. It's a gift, a final opportunity to connect and say, "I love you."

After breakfast, Mom returned to her bed saying, "Easter is the best day of the year." Then, she added, "The Holy Spirit is always waiting for us—all we have to do is ask. It's like picking up the phone." She spent most of the day in bed, comfortable and at peace, napping and then gazing out the window. She'd whisper, "Easter . . . Easter . . . Easter." She repeated the prayer that her mother had taught her, "Now I lay me down to sleep,

I pray the Lord my soul to keep. If I should die before I wake, I pray the Lord my soul to take."

I told my family I thought I might be witnessing Mom's last hurrah.

When the hospice nurse visited, she advised that my mother's symptoms indicated she would pass away within 48 hours. In the middle of that night, Mom awoke in pain. In a matter of minutes, she looked as if she'd aged 15 years. Her face and lips were pale, her eye sockets deepened, her breathing was shallow and, at times, stopped altogether.

Throwing away caution,
I removed my personal protective equipment
to lie on the bed next to her. I kissed her.

Throwing away caution, I removed my personal protective equipment to lie on the bed next to her. I kissed her. I told her how much I loved her. Mom was close to death, and it seemed as if she couldn't let go.

If a loved one shows difficulty letting go at the end of life, hospice professionals know to help give a sense of closure: "It's all right to go. Your work is finished. We'll miss you, but we will take care of each other. We will always love you. We'll be together again." Countless times I've seen these small but significant words release a loved one to a peaceful death.

While caressing my mom's hand, I *released* her. After a while she stopped breathing. I braced myself. Then—like rising from deep water, gasping for breath—her eyes opened wide as she looked at me and said, "Are you trying to kick me out?"

Later, I told my daughter that Grammy seemed annoyed with me because I gave her permission to go. She responded, "Annoyed is better than dead, Mom." As a large-animal veterinarian, she's seen her share of death. An amazing source of comfort and wisdom, she offered to fly to Illinois to care for her grandmother because "Mom, you're old." Nonetheless, I refused her thoughtful offer.

I began to dread the continued long nights, our slow walk through the Valley of Darkness. Keeping vigil next to her bed, I found myself praying constantly that God would end her suffering and let her die in peace. I felt selfish. I wanted no more scary nights with my mother on the brink of death. Sleep-deprived, emotionally spent, and feeling sorry for myself, I felt thrashed about like a shaken ragdoll. I'd been prideful about my hospice experience when I begged to take on this responsibility. Despite the love and support of my husband and family, I was scraping bottom, spiritually and emotionally.

Then, at two o'clock one morning, as I sat in my mom's wheelchair next to her bed, I opened an email from Dynamic Catholic in response to the pandemic. It contained a video entitled *Finding Calm in the Midst of the Storm* and told the story of the frightened disciples when they woke Jesus during a raging storm at sea. The disciples were terrified, but Jesus slept. The video emphasized that Jesus was full of peace when He woke and asked His disciples, "Why are you so afraid?"

Emotionally, I had tumbled down a deep, dark shaft and God rushed in to cushion my fall.

I still marvel at the grace of God in this perfectly timed message. Emotionally, I had tumbled down a deep, dark shaft and God rushed in to cushion my fall. He brushed me off and encouraged me to keep going. He whispered the reminder I needed: "Why are you so afraid?" By the power of the Holy Spirit, my faith was stronger and deeper in an instant. And by God's amazing grace, I finally surrendered and asked, "Lord, what do you think I should do?"

And by God's amazing grace,
I finally surrendered and asked,
"Lord, what do you think I should do?"

I feel ashamed to remember that my troubles always start when I shift my gaze from Jesus to something else: to myself, self-pity, social media, money, or any other shiny, attractive bauble. I know better.

I knew Mom was starting to feel better when she suddenly took an interest in Captain Tom, a 100-year-old former British military officer. In the midst of the pandemic, he'd raised millions of pounds for charity by doing laps around his garden using his walker. "Is he married?" she asked.

"God must have more work for me to do. Let's give more money to charity!" These words came after she successfully completed her first lap around her tiny kitchen with her walker.

My mother's former hospice nurse nicknamed her "the Little Miracle Lady." After spending 67 days with her in her home, she transferred to a rehabilitation facility to gain more strength. As of this writing, she has improved enough to move into an assisted-living apartment.

RESOURCES

When I returned to the Church, I was overwhelmed by what I didn't know. Initially, I could not relate to brilliant theologians and biblical scholars because listening to them was like trying to comprehend a foreign language. Below is a sample of resources that have helped me deepen my understanding of Catholicism while on my continuing spiritual journey.

WEBSITES & DIGITAL MEDIA

- "The Bible in a Year" podcast with Fr. Mike Schmitz, featuring Jeff Cavins.
  https://www.ascensionpress.com/pages/biy-registration

- Bishop Robert Barron Media Ministry. The wide-ranging ministry of Bishop Barron—whose Catholicism series is credited with countless conversions and bringing many fallen-away Catholics back to their faith—includes the following resources. https://www.wordonfire.org

  - Word on Fire Catholic Ministries. Daily online messages, including short commentaries on daily readings/Gospels.
    https://www.dailycatholicgospel.com/sign-up-page

  - Word on Fire YouTube channel. Teaching videos on the intersection of faith and culture.
    https://www.wordonfire/youtube

- Word on Fire Institute. Word on Fire films, study programs, and other digital resources. https://www.wordonfire.institute

- Center for Action and Contemplation. Daily messages from Fr. Richard Rohr. https://www.cac.org

- Center for Christogenesis. A spiritual organization bridging faith, science, culture, and community. https://www.christogenesis.org

- "Decision Point." A Dynamic Catholic study course created for confirmation students that helped me quickly rediscover the basics of my faith. Though not a teen by any means, I found the clear language helpful as I ramped up my faith. View for free in the Decision Point app. https://www.dynamiccatholic.com/decision-point-program-pack/DPNT-001-PP-01.html

- Dynamic Catholic. https://www.dynamiccatholic.com

- The Great Adventure Bible Study with Jeff Cavins, Ascension Press. This is a great "big picture" introduction to the Bible. https://ascensionpress.com/pages/the-great-adventure

- The Journey Home with Marcus Grodi. Features first-person videotaped stories about people returning to/joining the Catholic Church. https://www.chnetwork.org/journey-home

- Real Life Catholic. Offers a bounty of inspirational videos, including my favorite, "The Search," a riveting exploration of life's true meaning.

https://reallifecatholic.com and
https://coaching.reallifecatholic.com/thesearch

❧ Ron Rolheiser, OMI. Includes an inspirational-message
library composed of many years' worth of column
archives. https://www.ronrolheiser.com

❧ The Chosen. A multi-season narrative series about the
life of Jesus. View episodes for free in The Chosen app
and watch the Bible come alive.
https://watch.angelstudios.com/thechosen

BOOKS

❧ John Bartunek, *The Better Part: A Christ-Centered
Resource for Personal Prayer*, Ministry 23, LLC, 2014.

❧ Lee Strobel, *The Case for Christ*, Zondervan, 2016.

❧ Allen Hunt, *Confessions of a Mega Church Pastor*,
Beacon Publishing, 2010.

❧ Allen Hunt, *Everybody Needs to Forgive Somebody*,
Beacon Publishing, 2016.

❧ Rod Bennett, *Four Witnesses*, Ignatius Press, 2002.

❧ Jeff Cavins, Mary Healy, and Andrew Swafford, *The
Great Adventure Catholic Bible*, Ascension Press, 2018.

❧ Matthew Kelly, *I Heard God Laugh*, Blue Sparrow, 2020.

❧ Peter Kreeft, *Jesus Shock*, Beacon Publishing, 2008.

❧ Robert Barron, *Letter to a Suffering Church*, Word on
Fire Catholic Ministries, 2019.

❧ Kakadu, LLC, *Mass Journal*, Beacon Publishing, 2010.

❧ Matthew Kelly, *Rediscover Catholicism*, Blue Sparrow, 2014.

❧ Matthew Kelly, *Rediscover Jesus*, Beacon Publishing, 2015.

❧ Matthew Kelly, *Rediscover the Saints*, Blue Sparrow, 2019.

❧ Richard Rohr, *The Universal Christ: How a Forgotten Reality Can Change Everything We See, Hope For, and Believe*, Convergent Books, 2019.

❧ Lisa Brenninkmeyer, *Walking with Purpose: Seven Priorities that Make Life Work*, Beacon Publishing, 2013.

❧ *The Word on Fire Bible* by Word on Fire Catholic Ministries, 2020.

END NOTES

Chapter 1
[1] Dannion Brinkley and Paul Perry, *Saved by the Light: The True Story of a Man Who Died Twice and the Profound Revelations He Received* (New York, NY: HarperPaperbacks-HarperCollins, 1994).

Chapter 2
[2] Fred R. Shapiro, *The Yale Book of Quotations*, Calvin Coolidge Section, (New Haven, CT: Yale University Press, 2006).

Chapter 4
[3] Matthew Kelly, *The Four Signs of a Dynamic Catholic: How Engaging 1% of Catholics Could Change the World*, (North Palm Beach, FL: Blue Sparrow-Beacon Publishing, 2012).
[4] Ibid.
[5] Ibid.
[6] "A Universal Addiction," Center for Action and Contemplation Newsletter, December, 2019, https://cac.org/a-universal-addiction-2019-12-08/, accessed March 15, 2021.

Chapter 5
[7] Matthew Kelly, *I Heard God Laugh: A Practical Guide to Life's Essential Daily Habit*, (North Palm Beach, FL: Blue Sparrow, 2020).
[8] Ibid.

[9] For the section on the Prayer of Transformation, see Kelly, *Rediscover Jesus: An Invitation* (North Palm Beach, FL: Blue Sparrow-Beacon Publishing, 2015).

[10] Frank Sheed, *Christ in Eclipse: A Clinical Study of The Good Christian* (San Francisco, CA: Ignatius Press, 2020).

[11] Robert E. Barron, *Letter to a Suffering Church: A Bishop Speaks on the Sexual Abuse Crisis* (Des Plaines, IL: Word on Fire Catholic Ministries, 2019).

Chapter 6

[12] Donor solicitation envelope, The Dynamic Catholic Institute, 2019.

[13] Flocknote and Word on Fire Catholic Ministries, "82% of Your Parishioners Are Lukewarm. Here's how ENGAGE can help. . ." webinar, 10:47-26:09, accessed on March 5, 2021, https://engage.wordonfire.org/watchthewebinar.

[14] Oscar Wilde, "A Woman of No Importance: A Play" (London: Methuen & Company, 1908), 119.

[15] William Thomas Ellis, *"Billy" Sunday The Man and His Message* (Philadelphia, PA: John C. Winston Company, 1917).

[16] Kelly, *Rediscover Jesus.*

[17] John Baker, *Celebrate Recovery Leader's Guide* (Grand Rapids, MI: Zondervan, 2012).

[18] Kakadu, LLC, *Mass Journal* (North Palm Beach, FL: Beacon Publishing, 2010), Introduction.

[19] Kakadu, LLC, *Mass Journal*, Introduction.

Chapter 7

[20] Woodford, Jim, and Thom Gardner, *Heaven, an Unexpected Journey: One Man's Experience with Heaven, Angels, and the Afterlife* (Shippensburg, PA: Destiny Image, 2017).

21 NASB 1995 translation.

22 Ibid.

23 Robert Barron, "Daily Meditations from Bishop Robert Barron," Word on Fire Catholic Ministries, Mass email to subscribers including the author, December 17, 2019.

24 For this section see Matt Leonard (Director). (2011). "Catholicism" [Film; five-disc set on DVD]. Word on Fire.

Chapter 8

25 For this section see Howard Storm, *My Descent into Death: A Second Chance at Life* (Easton, PA: Harmony, 2005).

26 Kelly, *Rediscover Jesus.*

27 For this section see Kelly, *Rediscover Jesus.*

28 "Seeing Christ Everywhere," Center for Action and Contemplation Newsletter, February, 2019, https://cac.org/seeing-christ-everywhere-2019-02-13/, accessed on March 16, 2021.

29 Ibid.

Chapter 9

30 For this section see P.D. Eastman, *Are you My Mother?* (New York: Random House Books for Young Readers, 1960).

Chapter 10

31 *Catechism of the Catholic Church*, 2nd ed. (Washington, DC: United States Catholic Conference, 2000).

STUDY QUESTIONS
FOR GROUP AND INDIVIDUAL USE

Mass Confusion is about author Susan Dolan's 40-year journey away from and return to the Catholic Church. Maybe you, too, have left the Church. Or perhaps you haven't left physically, but you may be disengaged for a variety of reasons—you're bored, confused, alienated, frustrated, angry, or have unaddressed concerns. Maybe you attend Mass out of a sense of obligation or guilt. Whatever the case may be, these study questions are designed to prompt introspection, spark conversation, and enrich your understanding of the book's key messages.

1. Do you relate to the author's story because of your own experience or that of someone you know?

2. The author writes, "Looking back, I now see how God continually was weaving together for a far greater purpose the people, events, and experiences in my life, even though, for decades, I was oblivious to His subtle handiwork." Can you relate to this observation? Describe an event in your life that initially appeared negative but, in retrospect, turned out to be a blessing.

3. The author remembers her father teaching her to pray in kindergarten. What are your earliest memories of prayer? Has your view of prayer changed over time? How?

4. Do you notice a difference in your day with and without prayer? If so, describe the difference.

5. How would you describe your early faith formation? What would you change, if anything?

6. Despite the author's resistance to her faith in her youth, she described two experiences that left an impression on her. Do these experiences resonate with you? How? If not, can you recall other positive, Church-related experiences from your past? Make a list of them.

7. What does it mean to you to "Preach the Gospel at all times. When necessary use words."? Describe two examples.

8. Throughout the book, the author discusses hearing or sensing God's voice. For example, "It's time for a change, Susan. You've been working too hard; you haven't had enough time for me." Have you sensed God's voice in your life? If so, give an example.

9. Are you uncomfortable sharing stories about intimate encounters with God because of what people might think about you? If so, why?

10. Do you believe in miracles? If so, describe a miracle you have experienced, witnessed, or heard about.

11. Describe what the following quote by Saint Augustine of Hippo means to you: "Our heart is restless until it rests in you."

12. How can we discern our God-given gifts? What are your gifts? How do you use them?

13. Does the author's story help you share your own faith journey? Why or why not?

14. What lessons about life did you learn from the COVID-19 pandemic?

15. Have you ever felt desperately alone? Have you asked God for help in these types of situations? If so, did this change how you felt, handled the situation, or moved forward?

For a more detailed Study Guide go to
www.BerryTreePress.com/StudyGuide

ABOUT THE AUTHOR

Susan R. Dolan is a nurse, attorney, mediator, and health care consultant specializing in issues surrounding end-of-life care. She is co-author of *The End of Life Advisor: Personal, Legal, and Medical Considerations for a Peaceful, Dignified Death*, the American Journal of Nursing's 2009 Book of the Year. Susan appeared in the award-winning documentary *Consider the Conversation: A Documentary on a Taboo Subject*, served as a guest blogger for *The Huffington Post* (now *HuffPost*), and hosted ReachMD's radio broadcast. Susan lives in Park Ridge, Illinois with her husband, Steve. She visits Christ kitty every chance she gets.

Connect with Susan at www.susanrdolan.com

ABOUT THE SPEAKER

Susan R. Dolan shares her messages both virtually and in-person to church and civic groups and organizations of all sizes.

Keynote Addresses
Workshop Presentations
Retreats
Small Group Studies

Topics include:

❧ **Ending the Confusion:**
    Why I Returned to the Catholic Church After 40 Years

❧ **Is This All There Is?**
    A New Ager's Journey Home to the Catholic Church

❧ **Facing Death as Never Before:**
    A Hospice Nurse, COVID, and God

Check out in-depth topic descriptions at
www.BerryTreePress/speaker

For inquiries and to schedule Susan for your group, contact:
speaker@BerryTreePress.com